T0194449

Satan Don't Block My Way

Lillie Mae Hipps-Dickerson

BALBOA
PRESS
A DIVISION OF HAY HOUSE

Balboa Press books may be ordered through booksellers or by contacting:

Balboa Press
A Division of Hay House
1663 Liberty Drive
Bloomington, IN 47403
www.balboapress.com
1 (877) 407-4847

Print information available on the last page.

ISBN: 978-1-9822-2308-3 (sc)
ISBN: 978-1-9822-2310-6 (hc)
ISBN: 978-1-9822-2309-0 (e)

Library of Congress Control Number: 2018961460

Balboa Press rev. date: 02/27/2019

Table of Contents

TO MY MOTHER
DELLA MAE JONES

1

SATAN DON'T BLOCK MY WAY

Satan was standing at the door and he wouldn't let me
In God house
God was standing at the other side of the door for me
With his arms open to welcome me into his home
Satan have ruled my life for the last time
I am danger to fight with because I have God on
My side
I am giving you your last noticed to get out of the
Way
Satan don't block my way to God house you have
Block so many people way who want to come into
The house of God
Satan don't block my way
Satan get out of my way because I am walking
Into God house
Satan don't have no reason to hold me out here
In this world today so get out of my way and let
Me come into God house
Satan don't block my way

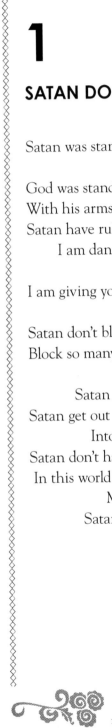

2

SET IN THE PEW

Sometimes you've go to church and your heart are
So cold
Satan walk in with you and you set in the pews with
A sad heart
God want you to give him your problem and heart to
Him
God will step into your life
God was set the pews aside of you when your
Soul hurt by some gossip that you hear in the
Street about you was not truth that hurt you so bad
Set there in church start you to wonder where did
The rumor came from and whom are spread them
In your heart you know that it not true

3

NOT IN THE CHURCH

Some of you don't come to church and give your life
             To Jesus
You said to your friend who may stop by for you to go to
          Church on Sunday morning not today
Someone had to preach over your soul when you leave this
            Old world
   Not in the church you step not in the house of pray
Your family and friend might belong to a church
    You are not in a church with the love of your family
    Jesus want you to serve him and worship him

4

A STUMBLING BLOCK

Satan cast a stumbling block in my way to
           God house
In my life Satan throw a stumbling block
Against med because I was in God hand
I went into the church with God and he given
Me the power to overcome and move the stumbling
           Block out of my way
In my stumbling block I will receive God seven
  Spirit of faith that he had laid out for me to
           Known his glory
Satan cast a stumbling block in my way to God
           Kingdom with his angels

5

I CAME TO THE MOUNTAIN

God is my shepherd when I need him to build me up
I came to the mountain
He will dwell in you and compact your love in your
Heart
Oh! I came to the mountain
God have mercy on me because I have sin at some
Point of my life
I pray for peace, faith, and happiness in my life
I came to the mountain
God is the shepherd in your life when you want to
Give upon life
You could be proud to have God for your shepherd
I came to the mountain

6

A THOUSAND SOUL

Your soul will not be destroyed in the Lord kingdom
The Lord will give you a chance to come to him
A thousand a soul out there need to be save in the
      Lord power
Please don't be lost I the lost in the Lord faith because
      He wanted you to live with his faith
I have a due season for you to come into mind
        Kingdom
A thousand soul is lost some were in the midst
      Of this old world
The Lord is given you a chance to come to him

7

GOD WILL NOT TURN HIS BACK ON YOU

God have created you to do his work for him
God will not turn his back on you
God want you to stand on his holy ground
Sometimes you might wonder away from God love
Your soul might wonder in a fore away place, God
Will not turn his back on you no matter what you are
Going through give him your hand and he will take
Your hand for you
God want you to cast his love all around your love
Ones
God will never turn back on you and the trouble that
You make be in with your family or friend
Remember God are there for you

8

SATAN GETTING OUT OF MY WAY

Devil I don't have time for you any more in my life
Devil my interested is not in you but in God
　　God are living down in my heart
Devil you are not a part of my life
Satan get out of my life
God are my salvation in my every
　　Moment that I live for him
　　Rejoice in the Lord
　　God will be your salvation
　　　God will keep you from fall in the hand
　　　　　　Of Satan
Devil I don't have time for you any more in my life
　　My life belongs to God

9

WHAT ARE YOU RUNNING FOR

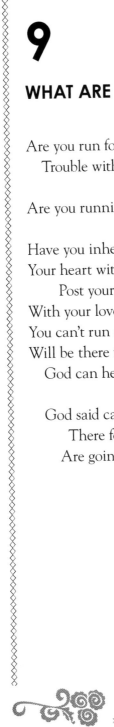

Are you run for your life? Because you are in
   Trouble with your family or you do not believe
       That God love you
Are you running from the law because you is in
       Troubles
Have you inherited the love of God? Why do you fill
Your heart with jealous and not love
    Post your time with God when you are sad
With your love ones. What are you running for
You can't run away from yourself or God because he
Will be there for you when you are in trouble
   God can help you when you need someone in your life
       What are you running for
God said cast your burden upon me and I will be
    There for you I will help you to face whatever you
   Are going through what are you running for

10

I FOUGHT AGAINST SATAN

I fought against Satan because he came with
His army of evil, jealous, backbite, adultery and
Sinning of the unclean spirit among the wickedness
In their heart
God heal the sick and the disease from among his
People
Someday he will reveal his power to all of his
Followers
I fought against Satan for my soul to go home
With God one day
I shall cast out Satan from my life because God
Have my life in his hand

11

SATAN WILL DEVOUR YOU

Satan don't have the power like God do
Someday I shall mourn for someone close
To me
I will let go of my evil thought in my life
Because God is in my soul
I will send up my praises in God
I will live in some heart's and soul one day
If you don't have God in your life, Satan will come and
Devour your soul up in his hands
Someday I shall go will God love beyond my joy in
My life

12

PLAYING CHURCH

So many preach are playing with God and so many
Of their congregation shall follow him in
To the devil hand
God want to deliver you from the devil and he
Will help you to face the temptation of the
Devil
God shall punish every living soul whom are
Playing church in his house of service's
and who step in his church of praise
Is you playing church

13

UNDER THE CLOUD

When you are fail by the give a pillow to lay your
Head on
God create a clean spirit under the c loud
My burden that have cast the brimstone into a
Fire well with a candle is burning in the wilderness
Of praises
Under the cloud that is better off when you have a
Fighting soul in God
God shall clean up your spirit with a little Faith

14

JEALOUSY AND ENVY IS IN GOD

Living in God soul is not jealousy or envy in the
Team of his flesh
I rather have love down in my heart and not hate,
Jealousy or envy
My instinct is in the focus of the living God
God shall be the fruit of my flesh and he is very please
With me
You shall receiver the gift of power in God faith
Wisdom in God spirit is not jealousy or envy in the
Valley of the living

15

GOD SET ME FREE

God rescued me and set me free in your rejoicing of prayer
I started out in a little house of God salvation
God came by one day early in my life and move me
From there into happiness
I want you to move from here and gain a little far in
Your life and don't escape me because I am
Your Savior and I shall set you free in my grace
I choose your life for you to follow in me
Your blessing is in me and my spirit of the Holy
Ghost is in you
God have set me free by his power

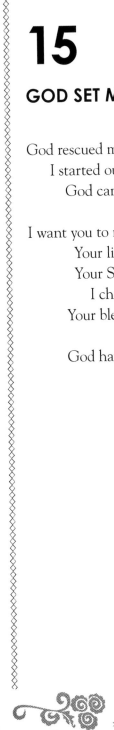

16

MY SOUL WILL NOT PREVAIL AGAINST

Credit my power to the wisdom of God in heaven
Is my labor prevail before him in a moment of time in
his kingdom for me
God build me up in time to plant my life with
His flower
My soul will not prevail against anyone who is in the
Hand of God
My grace is the reward in God love
God shall shield me in his peace and to the eyes of a
Needle
God have send me gold to hold onto in the house of
Treasure is in the heart of the one whom is in the
Eyes of my God

17

SPREAD YOUR FAITH

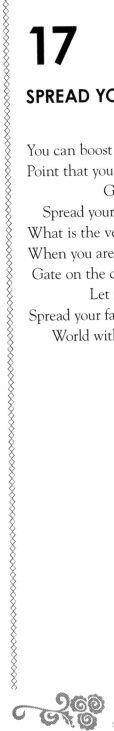

You can boost your feel with a great
Point that you carry in your heart for
God
Spread your faith in the world
What is the verdict in your soul
When you are standing at the golden
Gate on the camp ground will God
Let me come in
Spread your faith throughout the
World with the love of God

18

BEHOLD YOUR PEACE

Take off your old garment and the Lord shall give you
A new garment to wear to his party
My life will be peaceable in the beholding of the Lord
Tree of life
Behold your peace in the gate of holiness in the gift
Of living with the angel
Behold your faith with this generation to be making
In freedom
Take off your old garment and let the Lord clothing you
In a new garment to light up your spirit
Behold your peace
Behold your faith

19

YOUR PAYMENT IS DUE

You don't need a ticket to enter in the church and worship
With God
The preach shall support you with the love of his congregation
In the spirit
Is your payment of grace are due in the time for you to paid
Your tithes and offering in God
God is the called you to pay him with a song or a hymn from
Your soul
Your payment is due in season to the power of God
You don't need a ticket to enter in the church and worship
With God

20

A CONSTITUTION

A constitution of the law need to be amend in the
Kingdom
God shall make the constitution to be schedule in
His power
God shall hole the constitution of the law to be change
By his grace
God have schedules everyone to be rewarding by his
Angels in faith
The constitution of the power people need to be amend by
The power
God have the constitution of right in the world of power

21

I WANT A FULL TIME GOD

Are you full with the Holy Ghost Power
  Salvation is full of your spirit
I want a full time God and not a part time God
        God is with me all the time
God have hook in the gospel and in your voice for you to
        Sing with his angels
Are you full with the Holt Ghost Spirit
    God reward you with a full of faith and in his grace
    I want a full time God in my life and not a part time
        God
        God are with me all the time

22

PAY A FARE

Clear the air all around you in the cloud to restore
Your faith
Jesus pay a fare for all our soul with his life
Clear the way for me to be holy in the town of Zion
Jesus send out two of his disciples to mount of
Olives to preach in the town of Zion
Jesus pay a fear for all our soul with his life

23

A BODY OF GOD

Branch out your testimony in the church to follow
   You in the call of the Lord when your soul is cast
      Into a little well of precious water
A body of God shall be warm with your grace
      To receive the bridegroom
Branch out in the salvation of God army and
   Behold your mercy in the blessing of
      Rejoice

24

CALLED TO HIM

No harm shall come upon me when
     I called on him
Jesus send me one of his saint to serve
   With me in his home
In the evening hour I called to Jesus to
    Come into my heart for me to hold in
       The house of my meditation while I
         Sing to someone who need a song
To listen to in their soul
My spirit shall run among the wall of the
    Innocent soul who want to call on the
       Lord in their time of trouble so they
         Can be save in the spirit of Jesus

25

FULL REFUND

Will you want a full refund on life?
  When you expect to be send back into
    A big investment in Jesus blessing for
      You to be save
You can count on Jesus investment in your
Life to become holy with a full refund in
        Your soul
Someone life is less value to you without Jesus
    He wanted you to look up toward the blessing
        Faith in his salvation
Jesus full refund on your life is not a profit for
    You to be blessing by his faith

26

DOWN BY THE RIVER

There were many devils of disease in the flesh of
The sinner who wanted to be clean in the spirit
John baptized Jesus down by the river of Jorden so
We could repent our sin in the path way that we
        Have in our soul
Down by the ricer of Jorden Jesus immediately
Saw three brothers fish in the river and call to them
  Come and follow me and they went with him
      Down by the river

27

SHAKE THE WAVE'S

I was among my friend in the church
　　With the Holy Ghost work in the Lord
　　　　House of a strong wind blown through
　　　　　　The window of glory
The Lord stirring up my life in the river
　　Of my enemies who want to destroy
　　　　My life in the church with their wicked
　　　　　　Soul
The Lord brought my friend down very low
　　To the ground in their wicked life
The Lord shake the wave out of the water
　　For me to be holy in his thanksgiving
The Lord came and shake the wave out
　　　　Of my life with praises

28

BELIEVE IN RECEIVER

A believer shall beware of the spirit
        In Satan
        Stand up for a testament in the
           Sinful world
        A believe will not be blot out by
The blessing of the Lord
My life shall not be condemned by
        The power of Satan
I will be a witness to receiver the
        Blood in my soul
A believer shall come close to
        The Lord

29

WHY IS YOU LAUGH AT ME

Do you know that I am a child of the Lord
My precious blood is in his might power of joy
Why is you laughing
My life is a new drop of his precious blood and he
Shall lay his hand on me to receiver my burden in the
Light upon my hope in his salvation
Why is you laughing
Is you a child of God when you cast your faith upon the
Bosom of God
God want you to let his shine in your heart
Why is you laughing
Why is you laughing
My life is not fun and games to the saints of God

30

SAY NAY

Said nay to the people of God who is lost
Is you ready to follow God into the field of Jordan

My testimony is in the place to glorify the house
Of holiness
I was made cleaned in the mercy of God
Everything in my life came to pass in the city of
Galilee and God give me the power to rebuke
Satan out of my life
I went up to the house with God to prayer in his
Grace of peace
Let your nay said yes to you

31

A MIRACLES

A miracle may come your way in the spirit of the
Holy Ghost
The power is yours for the asking in God's name
God is the foundation of his children
A miracle shall deliver to you out of his way to the
Kingdom
The Holy Ghost shall enter in my heart and Satan
Shall depart from my life
One day my work will be finish down here
God shall lay out a miracle for me in his holy blood
A miracle shall make you hold in the wilderness
With the love of God

32

THE THRONE

I was sitting in the throne with God on my side to
       Keep me for rebuke him and his faith
God voice proceeded his seven spirit in his power
        Of the Red River that surround your thrones
           It was seven voices in the wilderness
I heard in the beast of the sea with eyes that
        Shine like lightning that come from God throne
         Of his flying power
I was standing in the door of God church knocking to
          Come in

33

CEILING

God design a ceiling with many of color for you to
Lock up in the church
The ceiling is make of glass design on the tiles
And the floor has marble stone design
In many colors
His saints decorate the church with many
Colors in designs of pebbles
God design a ceil for his church in salvation

34

CUT DOWN YOUR ENEMIES

The shadow of your enemies is not your friend in
                    The vineyard
Someone might cut you down when you are crying in
            The land of corrupt of the wilderness
Can you hear the spirit when your enemies
        Knocking at the door of the church
The spirit shall cut down your enemies in your
                        Life
The shadow of your soul shall fight off your enemies
                    Who are against you

35

I HAVE A CASTLE

My spirit is in the castle of time to understand
                    The wisdom
I have a trial in the castle with Jesus in mind
    My work is in the library of the castle so someone
        Can see my work in the class room with Jesus
I plant a garden in the yard of the castle with
    Grace to Jesus in faith with a bit of glory in
                    My heart

36

A OTHER DAY OF LIFE

God heard your voice in the wilderness
    He gave a day to the people to rest from they
                  Work
God limit his workday to six and he rest on the
              Seven days
    After another day of worked he came to you in a pillar
    Of glory and rocking you to sleep in his arms
God heard your voice in the wilderness called him to give
            You rest from labor
              Another day of rest in God

37

I MAKE IT THROUGH

I came through the hard part of my life with God
By my side
My faith is strong in God
God spoken to me in a pillar of dust
I make it through and gave my hand
To God
My life is with God now
He will hold me in peace
The doctor didn't know everything but God
Do, he wanted leave you along
I make it through with God by my side
My faith is strong in God
His power is strong in my heart
God is blessing me and you

38

MY SOUL IS FULL OF LIGHT

If my soul is lay in darkness of evil the Lord
  Shall show me the light in the world
The Lord light up the Lily of salvation in the eyes of
        Your warriors
The soul of the children was the light of the
        World
The Lord came out of the wilderness with a light in his
    Hand so the children could see his glory
My soul is full of light of God power
  The children of the Lord gather around to see the
    Wonderful light in all the world

39

A THIEF IN THE HOUSE

Jesus catch a thief in the house of praise and lock up
The thief in his jail of treasure to collect the gold
Coin in the heart of his congregation
Jesus turn over the thief to his govern at hand
Your thief is a partner of God
A thief is judge by God in the high places in
Manner of your spirit
A thief is in the house with my love for God

40

A DRUM IS BEAT IN THE TEMPLE

A drum is beat in your soul and your wisdom is a
      Happy time to praise God in a position way
               Of peace
There is more power in your voice when you give it
         To God and sing for his kingdom
A drum is beat heavy in the air for you to listen to God
  A drum is beating in the temple with all the angels
           Under the tent of glory
A drum is beat in the temple with God standing at
             The door

41

A LIGHT CONTINUE TO SHINE

My burden continued to light up my way to
                    God house
My labor is not in vain with power when God
     Examine my soul and all of us come together and
Eat at God table in the vineyard
A light continued to shine in your heart and your
     Blessing will come your way in God faith
My burden continued to shine in the sight of God

42

YOU SHALL REPENT IN MY NAME

Is you a witness in the wilderness when you repented in
          My name
When you repent in my name and be a witness to trust
In the wick of anointed in your heart
You shall not bear in the false power of his
          Name
Are you a witness for God when you repent in the nation
     The nation shall repent in the spirit with every
          Beat in your heart

43

IT IS DONE IN GOD

God shall cast the stone away from me in his spirit
Of war
Is done in the Holy Ghost
My flesh is better in God praise
My soul shall come out of prison
I will follow him down to the Red Sea so he
Can pour water on my soul from the sea of
Power
Is done in God faith
God said no evil word is done in him
God left me along for me to glorify him in the sacrifice
God shall cast the stone away for me in his reward on
Life
It is done in God power

44

A HOLY WELL

I went to the well for a drink of water when I cross
A mountain in Jerusalem and went all the way
To the home of the Lord
I met the Lord at the holy well with a glass of holy
Water of in his hand for me
I want a glass of the living water to clean my soul
With a little drop of his holy water from his
Holy well
If I drink a glass of that water from the holy well
I will live for even in his kingdom

45

GOD SPARATE YOU FROM EVIL

The flame of God name shall remain in your
Heart
When something is going crazy in your life God is all
Around you with love
God shall separate you from evil
Confess your sins to God and become holy in his
Sight of the water to clean your soul with
A light to bright your living in his
Eyes
God shall separate you from evil and you shall
Come to be happy in God

46

YOUR SOUL SHALL BE FILLED

Your soul complete with the Lord reward in the
Land of rejoicing
Lord have touch my life with his light to
Shine around me in a moment of glory
Your soul shall be filled with Lord unquenchable
Love and amazing power
Your blessing is apart of the Lord ministry to his
Hunger soul who need to be full of the
Heavenly bread

47

SEND ME AN ANGEL

Send me an angel to help me in due season in
    Time to separate my love from hate
The angel will not sleep in time when a trouble
    Soul come to the house of praise
The angel is make a melody in the heart of
    The saints
God send me an angel to help me to do your
    Will
Send me an angel to praise you in due season of
    My bosom

48

A HOLY GHOST PREACHER

The measure of a preaching come's with a precious
Moment of time
Jesus prepare his words to speak to his congregation
That is in the streets that have great faith with no
Where to laid they head at night or homeless
Jesus have lay his hands on the Holy Ghost preacher
Jesus powerful preacher is in the heart of the saints
That pour their soul out to him with the Holy
Ghost Praise

49

A BISHOP OF POWER

A bishop came by the house to received
      A bless in God
   Is you born in his blood with the Holy Spirit in you
If you are born in God precious blood your
     Spirit shall become clean with grace
A bishop shall beware of the evil workers
      In the house of God
A bishop has the power to speak in the
     Holy Ghost

50

PEACE IN YOUR SOUL

Beware of Satan who will come in your heart
      When you are in trouble at some moment
                Of your life
God shall hold Satan back from you because
      He will work with all of us in peace
God breath air into our nostril for us to live
      In peace of our soul
God want you to beware of Satan because
God known that Satan is danger to you

51

ANOINTED IS WISDOM

Bear the cross in anointed of
      His power
A name will bear anointed in the
        Holy spirit
I hear a voice call me in the kingdom
      And it was the angel with wisdom
        That appear before with joy
Bear the cross in anointed of his
        Grace
Let God arise with anointed power in
      Your soul

52

A GREAT VALUE

I learn a value lesson in God grace
    I shall remain faithful in the salvation of the
        Lord
God immediately show me a value picture of the
        Holy Ghost
The Lord is precious to me in time of my trouble's
The Lord have amazing voice of glory
The Lord send me a great value of his gift to
        The world
I shall claim your power in the hearts of mind
        Painful life
I chose a value lesson in the Lord kingdom of
        Wisdom

53

A BARGAIN OF FAITH

God went to the flea market to look for a stock in
                    The Holy Ghost
He fine a sample of faith at one table and hope
                    At another
A discount in his precious promise of pure oil in
                    The spirit
I bargain with someone for a little cup of
                    Grace
God went to the flea market to look for you to make
            Him a bid on salvation
He got a deal at a table of pray to save your soul
                    At a bargain price

54

A PATTERN OF LOVE

God shall show you the way to embrace someone who
Need a hug for you
God offer me a tender moment of his glory
In God pattern on life he is willing to renew
Your power in his faith
God shall cut out your pattern for you to be make
Hold in his prison of understand in the center
Of his love
My pattern is precious in God
My flesh is in God blood of praise
God shall cut out a pattern of
Love for me and you

55

OBEY GOD

I shall obey God in peace at all time
If you open your soul to God what will he
Fine in your soul to worship with him
My blood will not pass you by because you are
     One of my children in faith
I shall stand by your side when you are in
     Trouble and when you need me in the middle
        Of the night to come to you
I shall obey God with grace
     I shall obey God with praise in my heart and soul
        I shall over come god in time and obey him with
              Rejoice
My pains leave me with God helping faith

56

GOD DELIVER YOU UP

With God spirit wonder around down here you are
      In God holy faith
God deliver you out of the city and teach you with his
      Sheep of labor and preach to his shepherds
God enter to the village and healing the sick and
      Disease among his harvest in his glory
God deliver me up in his Holy Ghost and are scattered
      Abroad the thing that is not right in my spirit
God deliver me up in your wonder work in the
      Center of my voice to sing for you
My labor is not in vain with the grace in
      My heart

57

GOD AND THE DEVIL

The devil cast a unclean your spirit in front of you
God send you an angel to clean your soul with his
Holy power
God is against the devil power in your life
He will come to you and help you to face the devil
Because he had more power than the devil has
Tell that devil to go and leave you along
Because your soul is in the arms of the Lord
The devil cast an unclean spirit in your way to God
God shall stop him in his tracks
God send you an angel to clean your soul with his
Holy power

58

A BLESSING OF WINE

With a blessing on the third day of the week Jesus
    Stop by the house of a couple who was getting
        Marry they was had a big feast after the wedding
            In the city of Canaan and the wine ran out and
                Someone told him to fill six pots with water and
                    He turned the water into wine for the wedding party
                Jesus blessing the six pots of water and give a cup to
                        The groom to taste
                        The couple had faith in Jesus
                        A blessing in the wine of love

59

POUR OUT HOLY OIL

God have a box of oil in his chamber
　　All the little children's head was oil in holiness
　　　Some children went out shouting and tarry in the street
　　　　　With anointed oil
　　　　God pour oil into a vessel for his faithful servants
　　　　God went into the street of Zion and preach to the
　　　　　　Captain's and the house of host with all power in
　　　　　　　　His synagogues
Unclean heart God cleaning up the wick's one and
　　　　Pouring out oil on their soul

60

JESUS TOOK UP THE SHIP

Jesus walk upon the water when one of his
Disciples call to his in the spirit he answered
    Him back and said come I will hold you upon
        The water by my power and fear not I shall
            Help you walk on the water if you have
                    Faith in me
Jesus took up the ship and went on the other
    Side of the hill with his disciples by his side
Jesus took up the side in the wind and claim
              The sea by his power

61

DENIED BY SOMEONE

What shall a man exchange his life for when he
   Denied the spirit in his life
He can survive his life with the love from God
It is good to be made whole by the power of
    God
Someone came by and denied the faith in the
Job when God said follow me into the mountain
 And let your soul be a light for someone in the
  Vineyard and your soul will not be denied
    By God

62

EMPTY YOUR HEART

Can you contain your life with my beloved
    Children who I shall give them joy
            Empty your soul
There is nothing in your life if you don't have
         Time to show the lord faithful
         Empty your heart
The Lord empower you to speak to his generation
    To be heal with his judgment that dwell in
           Empty your life

63

PROOFED OF MY NAME

God have publisher everyone names in his book
                With an author
God print everything that we have done upon
        The star of a light so everyone can see
God have a text book with a hundred of pages
        To be turn one after another page of life
Your book tells a story of faith, joy, happiness
            And power in the life that you shall leave
                Behind you in God
God have publisher everyone names in the proofed to
                His world

64

A PLOT IN THE KINGDOM

The master of the holy plot came to you in a dream to
Tell you all about shaking the dirt from under your foot
My master came to heal the sick in the kingdom and
Pour out their trouble of the dust that mind
Master have in his will power
My master has a plot in his kingdom for me
And you

65

A UNDER GIVEN SOUL

I dwell on a seat with a few of mind
       Thing in my hand
I dream of heaven to repent of
    My sins in my heart
I was steadfastly by the Holy Ghost Spirit
   Of the fellowship of my soul
      With mind under given soul I shall hold
       The star close to my heart and the
          Love of the Lord
A under give spirit can stand in the light
      Of the Lord praise

66

FAITHS

I am here in faith
    I am here in power
        I am here in joy
            I am here in the sun light
                Shining down on my life
I shall see the angels in heaven one day
    The Lord shall be patience in my soul
For me to show him my faith in
                Him
I am there by his holy name
I am there in the spirit of the Holy
                Ghost
    I am there in hope
        I am there in happiness with the
                Grace in the Lord salvation

67

ACCORDING TO MY HEART

In the fornication of the temptation
    You will be burden down by the devil
        Spirit when Jesus leave your soul
           Along for three days
He shall never leave us along for one
        Minute in our life
According to the spirit in my heart I will
        Not fear Jesus die power to overcome
           The temptation of Satan quick salvation
               That dwell in my soul for the love of Jesus
            Because he always be in my life as long
           As I live in holy power

68

UNTO THE CHURCH

Jesus has and ear for you to hear him
    Talking to you in the church
I have received my Lord love for his
    Church by the power in my soul
My deed is not made of iron to be broken
      In my spirit of repented
I except all my salvation in the church
    That is written upon a stone that is a lite
Burden for me in the church when I receiver
  My Lord grace of his holy power
    Unto the church of work in the street when
      Your faith is broken down by Satan

69

CONTROL YOUR FAITH

Are you near to Jesus in your faith in the
     Time of control in your life in praise
The treat of the power is a part of the
        Spirit in you
Catch up in the power of the Holy Ghost
     In a deep hold that include in prayer
       Line of salvation
I live in a blessing moment of control faith
     In the center of the church
     Jesus hole my spirit in our life with
       His love for the church

70

MEADOWS IN THE SUN

As I run bare feet through the open field
In heaven Jesus shows me the path way
To a cool water stream
In the meadows Jesus restore my soul
        Of faith
In the meadows of the sun that came upon
      My life in salvation of the wind that
        Blown all around my sinful life
           In Jesus
In the meadow of my soul the sun
      Power came down on my life in
        A tender moment of life

71

PRAISED FOR EVER

All generation will praise him
   In the tender moment of
      Their lives
My praised is forever in the grace
Behold my glory to be a helper for
      Someone who need help from
        The Lord
In thy name my praise is everlasting
      In peace to the Lord
Behold my faith in the wilderness
      To come with hope in my heart
        With the love of the
        Lord
Praise forever in mercy
   Praise forever in love
      Praise forever in grace
Praise forever in the gate of
      The temple

72

TALKING IN THE SPIRIT

In goodness is unsearchable of my blessing in the
    House of righteousness that full my soul with
        Rejoice power that come down from heaven
    God shall praise us in the spirit when we have a
        Little talking with his faith in our heart everyday
    God shall not draw his hand from holding us up
        In the spirit when he is taking our soul with
                Hope
He is talking to us in the spirit of our heart

73

A EXTRA MOMENT

The Lord have deposit my personal life
    Into his bank of mercy
Extra moment of time I will shout
    My soul into heaven with the trait
      Of help from the Lord
In heaven the Lord have large chains
    Of companies for you to work in when
      You make contact him
In the building of gather of my soul into
      The Lord hands
I need extra moment in my life so I
    Can rest in the Lord arms
Extra moment of praise
    Extra moment of joy
      Extra moment of will power
I need extra moment of love from the
      Grace in the Lord

74

OWE JESUS NOTHING

I stand in the shadow of peace
    In a period of three week I shall be
Blessing in the moment of glory by
      The will in God
I owe Jesus everything in my life
I have pocket my faith in Jesus home
      With his Holy Ghost praise
Jesus shall open my heart for me so I
      Want owes then world nothing in his spirit
    I have a small investment in his power

75

WAS NOT SOLD

Cover up the hold in the center of your
      Life when Jesus rebuke the evil spirit
              Out of your way to his home
                One day
I was not sold into Satan hand by the
      Bread of my salvation
Jesus bring forth the good fruit into our life
      To not be sold by Satan because
He is full of evil thoughts
My life will not be sold into hell with so many
Lost soul in the world that is full of evil thought
      In their life
Jesus shall not sell you out from his Holy Victory

76

TELEPHONE THE LORD

An office of the house will call you and the Lord will
    Set up appointment for you to meet with him on
        The day of choose
In the ruler of your words in the holy city and the mail
Just went out of the Lord office of praise
The Lord is waited for your telephone call because he
               Want to talk to you
When you telephone the Lord and he shall asker you in
             About one hour
       Your faith could be with him at all time

77

THE HAIL ARE FALLING

Rebuke the falling hail in the rain from the
    Soul of the lost sheep in the vineyard
In the desert I wonder around the city
    In a smoke cloud that was full of
        Dark ashes in the vineyard
The hail is fall on the vineyard in the
    Form of rain in the kingdom from
        Heaven with love from God
The hail is fall on the vineyard in
    Mercy of God judgment in his spirit
        Of Egypt

78

I SHALL SET IN ORDER

Order to receiver my grace
I shall deliver you in a moment of
Precious blood order to see my house
    That is built in your heart
One day I shall set in order in the law
    Upon a stone that is burning in
        Your life
In my order I will not blame you
With the praise in your heart because
I will not judge you with the spirit in
   Order to deliver your blessing of all
The power that come out of your
Life I shall set in order some day
    In the future

79

DO I LOVE THE LORD

The Lord teach me of his mercy in
              Love
Evil spirit departed from me in the
     Commandment of the holy power in
My serve to the Lord
     Do you love God
My statue shall show you love for
     The Lord in righteousness
I have two branched of love on the tree
     Of hope one is time for a seed to grown
          And reaper by the hand of the Lord and
               Second is a word to receive a small
                    Rock of peace in the center of your
                              Soul
                    I love the Lord yes

80

I HATE NOT YOU

Someone quick my salvation
My lake run like a brook of holy
    Water into the sea of life
Nothing can not show me hate from
    Moment that the Lord came into mind
                    Heart
In the beginning of the judgment there
Is love and not hate for God
He shall hold my transgressor in
My work for the kingdom of love
    For God and not hate for the
            Congregation in the temple
                Of peace

81

THEIR BACK TURN

I search my soul as a witness in the
     Sevens of the Lord commandment
          In the delight of the world
              In peace
Nobody will turn their back on
     The Lord word in praise
My testimony is a part of the Lord
     Judgment that endure for everyone
          In the church
A precious miracle shall come to me
     When the people of the Lord turn
          Their back on me with great
              Peace in my soul

82

AT THE FOOTSTOOL

I worship at his mountain with his
    Strength down in my heart
I kneel at the cross in a holy way at
    His footstool with salvation
I make a joy noise in the house of
        The Lord
At the footstool my book keep turn
    The pages of my life with the precious
        Salvation in the church of the Lord
At the footstool of the Lord he shall open
    Up your book to your life and turn the
        Pages in his church of praise

83

RETURNED

A tastes of God salvation is a claim of his
      Continue love for you to returned to him in
            His power
God have returned a brimstone that burn everyday
      In someone life
Tastes of old blood is cast into a little hold upon a
      New church with my flesh in the church of
            The living
My old cheer is return into dust to be pour
      Out on the world in faith that the Lord
            Have send to everyone

84

CONSUME NOT

I was caught up in the cloud of the Lord
    With trouble all around me
The Lord cast my trouble into a tiny
    Bottle of faith with my daily
            Prayer
Something came into my life that consumed
Me into a sinful trouble world but the Lord
Was looking down on my life and save me
        From this trouble world
My life isn't consumed by the evil spirit
            In Satan
Consume not by the hand of Satan but
    By Jesus grace

85

LIGHT OF MY BURDEN

Bury your branch into a hold of daily
Prayer
A light shine upon the bosom of my heavenly
Father in heaven
He is the light of my burden in his north
Wind that blows through the middle of
My soul
I confess all my sins upon his bosom
When my burden is to heavy for me to
Carry all by myself
My heavenly father is the light of my burden
In heaven

86

WEARY OF THE SPIRIT

Jesus can blot out all your burning
   Spirit that built in your heart from
             Your life
My weary spirit is burning in the bosom
           Of Jesus
Some of you is weary of my faith in Jesus
           Holy power
I am not blind in Jesus eye when my joy
   Is full of his praise that I love in his
      Precious soul to be save by his power
        For us to come into his church with
          Salvation

87

MOVED OUT

A beast prevailed against me in the blood of
Jesus salvation
My soul entered in the house at a witness
Under the sun
Moved out of my way
I am looked for Jesus to come down and eat with
Me in a joyful time
In my life is worthy to be in a season of
Happiness
Moved out of my way
A blessed is precious in the book of praise to the
Nation with a golden cup of wine for you
To hold for Jesus one
Moved out of my way

88

FOUR SEALS

I have a penny of piece
    I hold a pair of faithful to rest my soul on
        The second tree of life
I saw three seals in the balances of my live
        For him
The Lord handed me the four seals in his spirit
    To be fill with holiness to open the
        Window of power
I follow ship with a tribe in heaven they have
    Two seals in each hand for me to be
        Measure in my spirit with

89

BRING FORTH JOY

Presidents and Senates are issues to the
      Rules by their our power in the government
         That is ignoring the working in the Lord
The Lord bring forth the votes in the land of
      The government that no one can
           Ignore
The Lord give you the opportunity to vote
      For the right person in government
The Lord bring forth the power into the
      Government to the people of the votes
         Rights

90

THE HOLY WALL OF JERICHO

Jesus sound his trumpet for the wall around
      Jericho to come down
The holy wall around the holy city fall
     When Jesus came in at the gate
The wind was great n the air when they
     Hear the voice of Jesus in the spirit
Jesus sound his trumpet the second time for
  His sheep to come to him with the might power
Of mercy in their soul when the holy wall
      Came down around the little city
         In faith

91

RESTORE WHOLE

Jesus restored whole life with a large part of your flesh
The wind arose up in the air and Jesus
    Rebuked the wind and made the sea claim
        In a manner of minutes
Jesus restored the whole faith in you and he shall not
    Suffered you with a little of his power when you are
        In his holiness of grace
Jesus shall restore your faith and cast out the unclean
           Spirit in your life

92

A SEASON WITH GOD

Jesus reign over my life in his
    Season of strength
I have a holy season among my enemies
To be judge in the power of God
My sin melted away from my life
In a tiny puff of smoke in my heart and
The precious spirit of my holy season
    In the air
I wait for my due season in heaven
    With a moment of peace

93

A HOLY GLASS

I hear a trumpet playing in my soul
With a victory march in heaven
A holy glass poured out a little cup of wine
So we can be rejoicing in the flood of the
Judgment in the Lord precious water
    Of our sin to be holy
In the presence of the Lord I shall
Hold up a glass of his holy wine to
    Become full of his grace with
      All the love that he left for me
        To come into the flood of life
        In his serve of praise

94

OUR LORD

In the early morning I shall
Praise our Lord as I serve him
With thanksgiving in a place
    Of peace
A little messenger came from your
   Heart into the spirit of the Lord
      With our testimony
I shall not fall into the hand of
   Satan, he is full of evil spirit
Our Lord have instructed Satan to
   Leave his saints along go to
     His home in hell
Our Lord have touch the life
   Of his saints to come home
     To him some day

95

REQUESTED YOUR LOVE

When I make a joyful song by the requested of the Lord
My life was judge by his holiness in the church
Requested your love
I endure my requested in love to reigned with a
Joyful moment that light up my way into
The home with God
Requested my spirit
When I make a better judgment in salvation as
I sat on the throne of God to be save in his
Holy power
Requested your righteousness in
The world
Requested your presence before the eyes
Of God

96

JUDGES TWO

God came with two wicked soul for them
  To rebuke their sin from them in the
    Hand of mercy
My vow was paid with power that came
  Down from heaven in a smoke puff
    Of faith for me to see around the
      Corner
I dissolved my trouble from my life in
  Judgment that pour out into a holy
    Bowl of peace in God hand to be
      Full of his mixture in his judgment
      Of two songs in my praise
      To be with God

97

MY FUTURE IS NOW

I shall donate my time to God temple and be
    Bless by his praise in my life
I sit impossible to be catch up in your dream
    Of the Lord future for you to come into his
      Faith as you wish for a good future
        With God
The tear that down from God when he is
    Crying in heaven soft for all of us to
      Be save by his son spirit and power
        In our future right now and not
      Tomorrow

98

CHECH OUT THE BALANCE

The Lord have give you change to be
Drafted into his program with extra
    Check to paid off your salvation in your
        Sin to the kingdom of wisdom
The Lord have check out the balance when he
        Draft you to come into his home of love
The Lord shall not play a game with your life
            Like Satan will
The Lord is real in everyone life and soul with
      Faith that's come dome from heaven in
          Glory

99

SHED YOUR BLOOD

Update your spirit as you shed your blood
     For the power in the Lord
You can be talented to refused Satan in
     Glory when you shout for joy in the
          Lord praise
I dwell with a small flock of the Lord host
     In the temple of grace
God shall help me to shed my blood in the
     Wilderness of peace to the nation
I shed my blood in the temple of
     The Lord for his love in my heart
     By his power in the sanctuary

100

FORSAKE ME NOT

God shall not forsake me in his
          Holy power
My face is turn up toward salvation
          In thee
My hope came out of the door
    Of all the mercy in me as my life
       Enter in the house of glory
God will not forsake you in the
          Church of praise
Forsake me not in the fornication
    Of life in God
   Forsake me not to leave the power
       In God
God will not forsake me in my faith
To the church in his love for everyone
       In the world

101

SAY NO TO SATAN

Final is not the mouth of the
        Holy spirit
Jesus said no to Saran as he entered in
His house of service in your faith to
        The wilderness
    Jesus shall say yes to you in the door
        Of his temple as you come into
            His home
            Jesus have a holy tent meet so you
                Could accept his love of other's
                Who shall show their love's in
                    The temple as you witness to
                    His angels in heaven

102

A EXTRA POWER

The Holy Ghost
Escape with all the
Power in you and my faith rushing
Down from heaven
An angel held you up in
Extra power that found all
Of the spirit in the world to be
Safe in your life with the grace
Of the Lord
The Lord will fill my soul with a little
Moment of his happiness for me to
Stand in the middle of the fire
That burned inside of your soul
The Lord have all his extra power
For you to be filled with joy of
Loving someone in your life

103

SEASONS OF WISDOM

Forever my glory shall be praise in
    The arms of the Lord
He finished open the doors of the
    Kingdom to anoint all the
        Soul in his house of service
In my seasons of his wisdom he came
    Down to the earth to show all of us
That he has the power in our soul
    To look down in our heart with
        His holy wisdom for our glory
        In the world as we walk in
        His shadow

104

MY TONGUE IS ON FIRE

From the house with the grace of the
   Lord my tongue is on fire for each
      Of you in the holy hill with the wind
Blown in the unlimited of time that filled
   My soul with a tiny piece of power in
         Heaven
During the rises of the holy fire down in
The middle of your soul shall burn for the
      Power in the Lord wilderness
My tongue is on fire for the war of peace in
       Your heart
Is your tongue on fire for the grace in his
power to explore your fire in his spirit
of love

105

CONCENTRATED ON GOD

Never quite concentrated on God
When you are a success in your dream or
In the life that is in God promise
Goal to the world
When do you start your job in the kingdom of God
To full your heart with a personal faith
In the church when you concentrated
On God
God want you to never quite his work that
You are doing for his church and your
Faith
Concentrate on God name in the church
Concentrate on God faith in holiness
Concentrate on God always in your life
Concentrate on God and never quite dreaming
About your life in the church of God spirit

106

RESPECTED IN GOD

Out of our bosom come respected for
       Other to be innocent
Your respected is on fire in the sanctuary
       Of the right hand of God
   God say respected what is in your heart to
       Hold onto with the fool in dream of the
          Moment of your spirit
         Respected in hope
Respected in the good that is in your
          Heart
       Respected your faith in God
        Respected is in your soul
In the portion of my flesh come respected
       To other in God
God want you to respect your life in
       Him and the church

107

BUT GOD

I might be author in the praise to place where
    My name is in the book of God
Because no one known me in the spirit of
            The church
I might be a legendry in a novel of power
    In the kingdom of God
        Accord to the glory in my life isn't chop
Out of wood in the country with my grand
  Mother during to some summer's
No one know me by the power in God
        Holiness praise of times
    No one know me but the grace of God
     No one know me but the love of God
      No one know me but the spirit of God
       No one know me in the power of God

108

MY BLOOD

My blood is in the
   Wisdom of the door
      Keeper as you march into
         My designer church's
Thy hope is coming
   Into the precious
      Blood of the son of God
The blood coming in at the
   Door of life to honor you in the garden
      Of grace so you can be a holy innkeeper
         Of all power to God who love you
My blood is drop down in a
   Tiny vessel to be full
      Of my precious tears

109

STUMBLED BY MY FAITH

A stone is set upon a block of my faith
        In the wall of the temple
God shield me from the burning sun in
                My soul
God increase my spirit in haven when he
        Heal my life with his victory
                Of salvation
I don't need a heavy power to be hold in
                The grace of God
        I stumbled in the church by the faith
                Of God
Shall you stumble in the church by your
                Faith and glory
I stumble in the door of the church with
        All the power in God

110

A DAY OF NUMBLERS

Yesterday is a number that will never come
    Against by the grace in the world
The word is promise in his number of glory
That he had make peace for you to hold
       Onto in him
My days is not a number the wing of him
       Doves in heaven
I dwell in a day of numbers of my time in
       The Lord
The Lord return my day to me in thine
       Remember of happiness
In my day of his temple is not countable
    In the spirit of his generation to follow
    Me into his serve of power

111

ANOINTEN AMEN

As I sleep God will buckler his wisdom in the
　　　Darkness of my soul to be save in his love
I have a thousand way to said thanks to God
　　　Anointed in power
My soul was brought before God in a dry
　Land of anointed of reproached in the field
　　　　　　Of mercy
　　Anointed-------------- Amen
As I wake in the morning God shall shield
　　Me with his wisdom of learn in all
　　　About his everlasting blessing in the
　　　Bottom of my heart
　　　Anointed-----------Amen

112

BARE YOUR FOOTSTEP

I shall associate with my footstep in Jesus
Board of prayer partner in the church with
The saint of praise
Jesus will bare the need in your soul for you
To become a member in worship to his
Congregation
He shall receiver you in a white light so you
Can become a minister in serve to him
Jesus will bare my footstep in his board
Of worship to his church of today in holiness
Bare my footstep in anointed
Bare my footstep in repent of salvation
Bare my footstep in the sand of the life
With Jesus
Bare your footstep in the time of praise
To the church

113

REWARDED OF POWER

The faithfulness is in my power of crying
     In all the kingdom
I hold onto a strong hand in battle for
     My holiness in God
Peace in reward to all congregation as
     Their burden came into a place
          Of glory
In reward to my life is not a stranger
     In the power of God
I shall be satisfied in God house
      Of faithfulness
God committed me into his house
     Of holiness in praise of time

114

CRYING IN THE WILDERNESS

As the sun came up with the shadow all around
　　You that is peel down on you from heaven
God is looking out for you to be bless upon
　　　　　His Peaceful Mountain
　　　　　Crying in the wilderness
I am in the body of power s one soul wo is cry
　　　　Out into the land of forgiven
　　　　　Crying out in the wilderness
God have all our fault in his holy palms of his
　　　Hand for us to come to the peaceful
　　　　　Mountain with grace in our lives
　　　　　Crying in the wilderness
　　　　　　Crying in the wilderness

115

TAKE AWAY

Draw my life out of Satan hand and reproached
     Me in thy spirit of your holiness
My life is take away by the grace in you my Lord
    In the middle of my soul you came into mind
       Salvation with peace
I know that you shall not take me away from
     The temple of praise in your kingdom
The Lord shall draw me out of the way of
        Satan
The Lord will help you to draw your life from
    Satan hand because he is all way with
       You

116

I AM POOR

Jesus assembly all his poor together to
        Become rich in his faith
I shall serve all the poor and rich in his spirit
        To testify of my wealth in Jesus
I am not poor in Jesus word because he will
        Male all of us wealth by his power
My life is valuable to Jesus in money, houses,
Cars, clothing and boats didn't make you
        Wealth in his power

117

THE PROUD OF FAITH

The Lord want you to be proud of your
        Faith in him
When you are proud in your heart and you might
        Yield to the strong voice of the Lord
Be proud of yourself in your life with the
        Lord
Fear not in the proud plug of your salvation
    Because the Lord shall open your heart
        To the church when you are close
            Off from his congregation

118

MAY REJOICE

Someone attended to the rejoice in the
      Kingdom of wisdom
I shall live among all the nation in
      Peace
Jesus stretched out his holy hand in
    Lovingkindness in the due morning air
      That blow all around our life in his
        Grace
I cry with my voice to Jesus in rejoice
    Of the salvation in my soul
  You may rejoice by my spirit
    You may rejoice in the power of the Lord
      You may rejoice in hope to all generation

119

PURCHASE A NEW LIFE

I plague my old soul for something new
         In the eyes of Jesus
Love faithfulness is purchase for my old
     Life on the cross in a shining
         New star
Jesus purchase me a new life when I prayer in
         The wilderness
I shout for a new dance in heaven
   My labor is old in the spirit of my heart
      I plague my salvation into the house of blame
         Of less soul to be holy in Jesus
Jesus will hold fast to my new life in the door
      Of his love for him

120

GOD BILL

What are God bill to you to reading your bible
　　　Every day as you serve him
God bill show you how to live in this world
God bill are calling you to love his people who
　　　Need you in their life
God bill are to service his church every day
　　　Of your life
God bill is not cloth, car payment, rent your
　　　Telephone or electric bill
　　God bill are to service him
God bill are for you to follow him to church on
　　　His day of worship
What is God bill to you it is to pay your title
　　　Or mission when you go to church
　　Can you striving toward God bill with
Your heart when you have a little faith with
　　　In yourself
You can make a differ in someone life
　　　Who need God today
God bill is in the glory of his love that he had
　　　For you

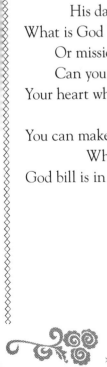

The elder

I came to the mountain

Printed in the United States
By Bookmasters